Setting Boundaries

To repel bullies and dissolve codependence

Ann Ford, M.S.

Please see YETItips.com for the latest in practical self-help and abuse recovery books.

ISBN-10: 978-0-692-23539-3

Contents

BOUNDARIES To Protect Yourself

- TO REPEL BULLIES
- TO DISSOLVE CODEPENDENT BEHAVIORS

WHAT IS A BOUNDARY?
A boundary is: a LINE that marks a LIMIT.

Most members of Adult Children of Alcoholics and other dysfunctional families grew up lacking secure boundaries. Less than 25% of the U.S. population grows up in a "safe" environment, since the U.S. has high levels of violence to adults and to children.

Most of the parenting examples ACoA members have experienced, were unstable, interrupted, aggressively competitive, physically harming, emotionally humiliating – or in some major ways, environments that:

- Did NOT protect children or erect boundaries around them for their safety.
- Did NOT demonstrate by example to children, how to be ASSERTIVE or how to defend themselves, such that-
- Most kids developed slightly "abnormal" ways of defending themselves out of their fear of punishment or abandonment, and so most ACoA members have functioned with a lot of fear and rage suppressed inside, while OUTWARDLY pretending to be very "accepting" people.

Kids did not grow up SEEING how to build HEALTHY BOUNDARIES for themselves, and did NOT have confidence instilled that they were WORTHY of PROTECTING by boundaries.

Healthy intimate relationships co-exist (they're not enmeshed).

Person A - loves self, is honest, trusts self and B

Person B - loves self, is honest, trusts self and A

With love between two people, each still has their "self" boundary.

What challenges we face building boundaries

The founder of Adult Children of Alcoholics, Tony A., said that ACoA kids have been taught to survive frightening childhoods by going into a "freeze" position whenever there's conflict, in order to not get hurt or yelled at. Tony A. says that ADULT ACoA members CONTINUE to go into "freeze" position whenever they are confronted with CONFLICT.

The four most basic emotions are: Mad, Sad, Glad, or Scared. Adult children of alcoholics "freeze from being scared. Most ACoA members need to learn:

- That adults know how to regulate ALL their emotions.
- That anger is a natural emotion that it is good to use at specific time to PROTECT YOUR BOUNDARIES.

Because ACoA members have been so frightened growing up – or abandoned – with the result that many of us have the reactions of Prisoners of War camp escapees, we need to master movement, meditation, yoga or meditative movement, and emotional expression – to DISPELL the stored fears of our childhood experiences that still are stored in our bodies.

We learn to regulate emotions like an adult, by experiencing them. Watch some movies to release your feelings. Watch a **funny** or **inspiring** movie like:

- *"Switch" or "Last Chance Harvey"*

- *"Our Idiot Brother"*
- *"Airplane"*
- *"Blades of Glory"*
- *"The Help"*
- *"Martian Child"*

Watch a **sad** movie like :

- *"Running With Scissors "*
- *"People Like us"*
- *"Terms of Endearment"*
- *"The Hereafter "*
- *"My Life as a Dog"*
- *"Prince of Tides" (Nick Nolte)*
- *"This Boy's Life" (Leonardo DiCaprio and Robert DeNiro as the cruel parent.)*

Once we (1) become familiar with expressing ALL our emotions – even ANGER – since it helps us protect our boundaries, then we can move on to learning other vital skills. We need to follow what one of the introductions of the RED BOOK says we need to learn – what the RED BOOK writes about a lot – ASSERTIVENESS. The ability to face conflict and NOT "freeze," is one of the major skills everyone needs.

You can take an "Assertiveness Course" to:

- Learn how to NOT "freeze", and

- Learn how to respond ASSERTIVELY to conflict.

- You can practice the techniques listed in this section, and master the SKILLS.

- After assertiveness, practice TRUSTING yourself and VALIDATING YOURSELF.

- After you build A STRONG CORE IN YOURSELF, you can learn how to build our OWN HEALTHY families.

STOP FOR A MOMENT:

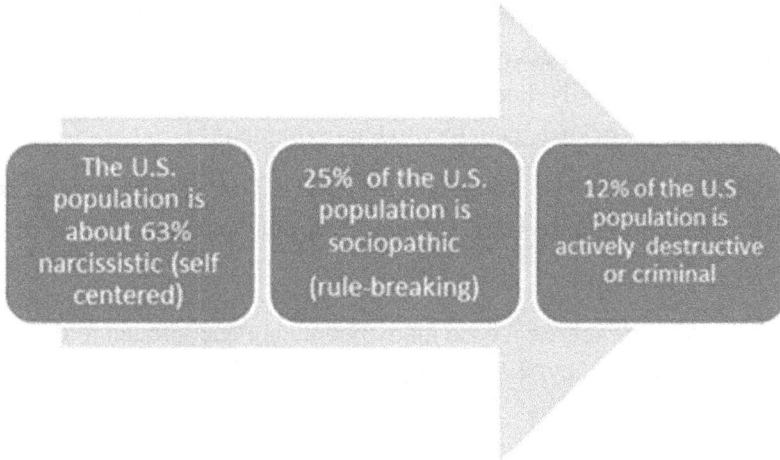

The U.S. population is about 63% narcissistic (self centered) → 25% of the U.S. population is sociopathic (rule-breaking) → 12% of the U.S population is actively destructive or criminal

The U.S. promotes a "me-first" culture

The U.S. culture style, and the fact that the population has high numbers of self-centered people, results in (1) poorer parenting skills than some other nations, and (2) generally low compassionate caring, compared to some other nations.

This is not intended as an attack on U.S. parents. Every country is different. Bosnia is a LOT more violent than the U.S., with higher rape and murder rates. Japan is 130th as violent as the U.S., Mexico is also violent to its children and adults, and has a high murder rate. Every country is different.

The U.S. places such a VERY HIGH EMPHASIS on aggressive competitiveness in the workplace, that many parents find they can barely keep their heads afloat economically, let alone do an attentive job parenting. It is the way that the nation IS. Things have improved since the frontier days of lynch mobs, with social services protecting some children, and with national mental health days focusing attention on how the nation has to change.

Other countries are leading the U.S. into better behaviors. Denmark has practically emptied its jails and has a very low crime rate now, and used to be as bad as the U.S.. We can learn from them. In Thailand, the emphasis is on COOPERATION between people, even at work, not COMPETITIVENESS, and the U.S. can learn from that. After a tsunami in Thailand, the national government refused to let a single baby be adopted by an American family, because the Thai people did not want their baby "citizens" raised in such a competitive environment.

The U.S. is a ROUGH country, and it was TOUGH on your parents, and it was TOUGH on you. NOW it's time to FIX the damage.

TIP:
The U.S. is super aggressive, so many people are encouraged to do forms of bullying so that they "Feel taller when they make others feel smaller."

Tell-Tale Clues That You May Not Have Strong Boundaries

Professional criminals who mug people, have been interviewed about how they select their potential victims to mug on the street, to take a wallet or a purse. They describe certain characteristics that make someone look like an "easy" target:

- Potential victims are walking alone – if you have a partner you are not an easy target.

- Potential victims do not seem to be aware of their surroundings – they look down and are inobservant.

- Potential victims seem to have low energy or slow walking – they don't seem physically STRONG.

- Bullying and victimization boils down to INTIMIDATION. Your will is DOMINATED BY someone else. Even the word INTIMIDATE – in Latin – means "make afraid". When we are victimized we have also given the abuser UNDESERVED trust – and put ourselves too CLOSE to them, so they could hurt us.

REMEMBER:
Most of us meet bullies of the common and plentiful variety – most of us do not meet predators. All the methods mentioned in this guide, for dealing with "common" bullies, do NOT apply to PREDATORS. Predators are ruthless sociopaths/psychopaths who operate ILLOGICALLY, so you cannot reason with them.

TRAIN YOURSELF TO BE STRONGER AND FACE CONFLICT

Memorize a script to say to invasive people:

- "Good luck to you – but I can't help. NO! I can't help you."

- "Do you know that what you just did (or said) would sound VERY rude to most people? You could be BADLY embarrassed. (Bullies want ADMIRATION – not to be embarrassed.)

- (If you have brought a friend or partner with you, turn to them and speak.) "This seems like a conversation that is meant to be mean, let's go over here and find something else to do." (Or turn to the put-down person and say) "Excuse us, we have to be somewhere else and are going now."

- If you are walking by yourself – day or night – carry a metal cane – you can buy them at the drug store – and swing it aggressively as you walk. It will transmit someone who is AWARE and ARMED. Also, carry a personal alarm and set it off EARLY – don't be shy.

Does Your Body Language Say "I'm Easy"?

One fellow was exiting a coffee shop with his sister one morning as they planned to talk and walk through a park. This crazed guy came up and started talked at the brother and shouting: "Why won't you talk with me? You think you're better than me? You're just an asshole! You're an asshole!"

Then the guy turned and ran off. The sister had told the brother not to talk with the guy, but the brother had tried to speak to him politely. A few minutes later they heard a car start noisily, and the "crazy guy" revved his engine in his little red car and drove off. He had gotten what HE wanted that morning: the opportunity to scare and put-down some people – so he had PLENTY of energy for the rest of HIS day.

The brother said to his sister; "What is it? Is there something tattooed on my forehead?"

The sister said that YES, there was a body language that kids from abused families sometimes give off – that they expect or will TOLERATE some abuse from other people. This brother also had a ring of white around his iris – left over from childhood fear when he was beaten once a week – for no good cause.

Past fear and abuse leave tell-tale traces on your body

When prisoners of foreign wars return from battle, there are tell-tale symptoms of the fear that they have lived under. There are very similar symptoms that exist for kids who have grown up as "prisoners of domestic wars".

Only Canada treated – routinely – all returning POWs with LIFETIME supplements of B12 injections, since their nerves had been completely destroyed from their experience being dominated and threatened. In present times, the world's war victims who have been tortured, are accepted free for treatment, in Denmark. There are kept in the country, in a remote, quiet

11

place, with hours of gentle massages administered, until the terror that has lodged in their bodies – is eventually released.

If you can imagine how depleting and spirit-destroying it is, for an ADULT, to be enmeshed and try to survive day after day, when an adversary seems to be weaving a web of evil to consume you – you can imagine how terrified a child grows up, under similar circumstances.

Tell-tale signs include:

- Not looking people directly in the eye.

- Lowering the head, as if trying to avoid a slap to the face.

- Standing with shoulder slightly curved, as if to protect the chest from being hit.

- A habitual posture of arms crossed over the chest – a DEFENSIVE posture – pre-argument or anger.

- Using the threat of blowing up – angry tantrums – to control others from interfering with them.

- Having a rim of white showing around the iris in the eye – like a frightened horse before it runs away.

- Hyper-vigilance and often hyper-hearing, in chronic eavesdropping.

- A flinch factor at ANY degree of noise – small or loud – any sudden surprise or abrupt movement.

- Dislike of being touched by other people – particularly strangers, and may not shake hands. (It's an illness called "sensory defensiveness").

How to Recover and Build SELF VALIDATION

What you can do to repair your injuries and BUILD BOUNDARIES:

- Learn to say "NO!" with no justifications, and learn other assertive phrases & actions.
- Practice buying something and returning it to the store – that's assertive.
- Do self-protective actions – including avoiding unsafe people.
- Call up your ANGER and use it at people who are invasive – that's a boundary.
- Tell people how much or little of YOUR time, they can have – YOU direct how you spend it.
- Learn to recognize different levels of trustworthiness.
- NO LONGER give UNDESERVED TRUST to people, like co-dependents do.

Cry at sad movies until you can't cry anymore. Sometimes it will take more than an hour. "Terms of Endearment" is a good "'weepie". Once the emotional "baggage" is released, you have access to more of your STRENGTHS!

Arrange to have a partner to go with you when you have to do something scary or go somewhere where there are bad people

Feel free to tell someone that: "I'm feeling manipulated and intimidated here, so I can't continue this," and leave.

Look for the silver lining – something of beauty in every day – clouds overhead – a butterfly or bee zooming by – and remember feelings of sadness, anger and fear do NOT cancel out the GOOD of life, and that there are silver linings.

Do not feel "pity" or feel "sorry" for people you say "no!" to.

When you co-depend with someone– you DEPRIVE them of growing up in all the ways that we are to intended to, to be mature adults.

Every Single Day Increase Your Self Validation

SAY TO YOURSELF EVERY MORNING AND EVERY EVENING:

- **You are kind.**

- **You are smart.**

- **You are loved.**

- **You can make mistakes.**

- **You are valuable.**

- **You are a worthy human being.**

EMDR and EFT

EMDR has been used successfully on Post Traumatic Stress Victims, in less than a few weeks. By teaching a person to follow another person's moving finger, or by teaching a person to tap their knees alternately – you are *interrupting a mental habit* of emotionally welling up to a painful thought, or memory. You are *changing the focus to another sensation*, and lessening the impact of the anxious thought or memory – which is how the trauma is reduced.

Using the EFT – Emotional Freedom Technique (free on the Internet), one learns to tap the eyebrows and cheekbones and hands, in ways that ALSO distract from the anxious thought At the same time, you say to yourself affirming statements such as "I'm an adult now, I have skills to handle this. Also, walking up a steep hill, pulls blood to the lower body, and a person calms down.

BULLYING and What Drives Bullies

Bullying is an activity that gives the bully a set of feelings that they lack – often from having been bullied themselves. The bully looks to feel:

- Respect from the peers and the audience.

- To instill fear in peers and audience if he/she cannot inspire respect.

- To feel the "high" of dominance (hormones of testosterone, adrenaline and dopamine may all be involved).

- To get a REPUTATION for being "strong" – in that the bully feels taller when he/she makes others feel smaller.

- Bullying can be "anonymous" on the web – so the incidence of cyber bullying has HUGELY INCREASED – with the power to slander that old-fashioned gossiping used to do. When there is anonymity, the bully "loses" some of the high of being PERSONALLY admired, so on-line slander/libel can increase and there can be more and more attacks, than there would have been physically.

There are degrees of bullying. Sometimes a person will progress from the first stage of bullying – showing off to an "audience' to get a "dominance"' high, and go all the way to the ultimate form of dominance and kill someone – that's a psychopathic predator.

Bullying I.	Bullying II.	Bullying III. - Predator
Oblivious to what others feel – loves doing putdowns	Covertly mean – gossiping – some malice	Overtly cruel – malignant narcissist destruction

The categories of bullying

The first two categories of bullying can be confusing, because **Bully I** can be capable of *receiving* love from other people, and may be capable of giving some amounts of it. **Bully I** is limited by the degree of narcissism they live with (self-centeredness).

Bully II is of the Malignant Narcissist category, which due to childhood deprivation or other cruel experiences, is solely intent on their own survival and their own feelings of being 'powerful'' or "dominant", and they are incapable of loving another person.

NARCISSISTIC PERSONALITY DISORDER

From the DSM-IV (Diagnostic and Statistical Manual of Mental Disorders) pg. 714:

> *"DIAGNOSTIC FEATURES*
>
> *The essential feature of narcissistic personality disorder is a pervasive pattern of grandiosity, need for admiration, and lack of empathy that begins by early adulthood and is present in a variety of contexts."*

Among **8** tell-tale features are:

- "is uncomfortable in situations in which he or she is not the center of attention"
- "displays rapidly shifting and shallow expression of emotions"
- "shows self-dramatization, theatricality, and (unprovoked) emotions (like tantrums)"
- "considers relationships to be more intimate than they actually are."

From the Dictionary Of Psychology (by Arthur & Emily Reber):

> ***NARCISSIST*** *– "... development characterized by a love of self that PRECEDES, IF NOT PRECLUDES, LOVE OF OTHERS.*
>
> *The neurosis causes the person to have an excessive need for admiration and attention, and inappropriate emotional reactions to the criticisms of others. It is a neurosis characterized by such excessive self love (following a childhood emotional injury of neglect) that NORMAL LOVE FOR OTHERS IS IMPOSSIBLE."*
>
> ***MALIGNANT NARCISSIST*** *– a personality disorder characterized by "... suspiciousness to the point of paranoia, feelings of self-importance, and sadistic cruelty accompanied by a complete lack of remorse."*

16

When Bullies and Helplessness Force Codependence

Narcissists often cause codependence, using charm or anger to make others obey them.

- ONE – Children often learn CODEPENDENCE at home because it can be the MISSING PIECE of behavior that an OVER-CONTROLLER (addict-adult) wants – the over-controller can get their needs MET and obeyed, by a co-dependent – someone dependent upon them. This can also occur among ADULTS when one adult has disproportionately more power or money or control, than another.

- TWO – Codependence can be a form of COVERT CONTROL in reaction to what a child senses is an OVER-CONTROLLING person. The child – and later the adult child - attempts to wrest control back to themselves by pleasing others – it is manipulative and a child's way to self-defend yourself, without being attacked.

When Emotional Drives Turn to Cruelty

Human emotions fulfill different uses in different circumstances. People who escaped over the Berlin Wall or escaped from concentration camps, used their most ruthless and cunning skills – and sometimes had to kill people to escape – in order to survive. There are circumstances under which almost anyone will kill another person, including the obvious one to kill for their own survival and self preservation.

What about the violent bully – the predator?

There are vindictive criminals in our world, who have behaved badly for many years, and who felt that they had no chance at a better life.

Although the predator has no trust in other people – or because of having no trust – the predator may be highly charming and skilled at manipulating others. They can get helpers or followers sometimes, by weaving a web of evil around a person. But usually, the predator has been cruelly treated growing up, trusts no one, is attached to no one compassionately, and so is criminally cruel.

Emotional drives

There are many variations on the basic human emotions and human drives, but according to the in-depth research done by William Glasser, M.D., there are FOUR very deeply conditioned and motivating drives. Some of these cause cruelty and some of these cause deep compassionate caring.

Generally, the more "playful" – and callously regarding other people as playthings – attitude combined with a HIGH drive to be competitive, and powerful, and have high personal freedom (be BEYOND society's (rules) combines to fuel the drive of greatest cruelty.

Four drives – some cause love, some cause cruelty

POWER People who choose power can be violent, cruel, and can be MALIGNANT BORDERLINES	**FREEDOM** People who choose freedom can be callous
FUN AND COMPETITIVENESS These people can be HIGHLY self-centered – they can often be MALIGNANT NARCISSISTS	**LOVE AND BELONGING** These people often have more compassion for other people

Bullying children at home

The only preventative to bullying or cruelty drives at home, are if the caretaking adults have HIGH drives for Love and Belonging, which cause kindness.

If an adult is under the influence of alcohol or other drugs, the self-centeredness, the drive for 'fun' and 'power" and "freedom" – all combine to make a VERY inconsiderate or MEAN person while under the influence. If this person is parenting, they are likely a cruel parent.

Bullying done "at home" or in the privacy of a parent's home or a foster home – is extremely difficult to restrict because:

- The official "guardian" of a child has temporary or permanent legal rights that the children do NOT have.

- The official "guardian" or AUTHORITY FIGURE, has the power to inflict an atmosphere onto children, of being in a Prisoner of War Camp – or like being kidnap victims.

The official "guardian" may be:

- Low on compassion,
- High on aggression,
- Very depressed, or an addict – all of which leads the "guardian" to seek out the easy-to-get dominance "high" of doing a put-down, or abusing a child or any household members.

BULLYING AMONG CHILDREN, COMPARED TO ADULTS
Bullying in schools –

Bullying in schools is often impulsive and opportunistic – completely unplanned.

The incidence of bullying young children – younger than junior high level, is 3 times higher than the level of bullying that occurs in high school.

In school life (and in adult life too) – bullies take advantage of spontaneous opportunities – seeing someone alone – not being with a buddy. The opportunistic bullying is likely reduced in high school because so many high school students:

- Have learned a few assertiveness skills.
- Many high school students travel in twos and threes, so are not as easy to target, as is a single kid.

Bullying among adults -

Bullying among adults is also impulsive and opportunistic, much of the time.

In road rage or regular driving when people cut drivers off – it's impulsive and opportunistic, as is cutting in line at the post office, or Federal Express, or coffee shops and other locations.

When adult bullying of adult children is deliberate

There are also "campaigns of bullying" that are deliberate – not opportunistic – frequently among employers who are not mentally well. But the most frequent source of bullying campaigns comes from "loved ones" – former boyfriends, mates, spouses, or most particularly among older family members who are not mentally well and need professional help.

A parent who has been raging at his or her kids for years, often resents an adult kid wants to be treated better – and gets MORE enraged! Some parents begin to physically slap or hit their adult kids, when they hadn't previously, because their rage has increased over time and they have fewer outlets for their rage to be released – as their social contacts decrease with age.

Adult children can find themselves on the receiving end of as much or more rage, than they experienced in childhood. The adult child may still be allowing this abuse – giving UNDESERVED TRUST to this former love or relative.

Some adult children decide to severely limit contact with such familiar abusers, or simply to cut and eliminate contact, when the raging "authority figure" in their family, does NOT get professional help.

Many times the raging adult has been to M.D.s for other ills, and has been advised to take anti-depressants, or other medications, to calm down their high aggression. M.D.s can see in their behavior and by their blood pressure that they need medication – and the parent or guardian REFUSES to take the meds. They do NOT want to change, because they will lose their satisfying, familiar ways of behaving.

Impact of bullying on adult children of alcoholics and dysfunctional families

People who have experienced bullying done "at home" or in the privacy of a parent's home or a foster home by a parent or official "guardian", have often grown into adulthood:

- Finding it feels most familiar being around authority figures who are able to inflict an atmosphere of being in a Prisoner of War Camp.

- Having behavior habits that make them respond like victims, rather than survivors, and they may internally still feel they have to respond to requests or demands, like being kidnap victims.

- Being unaware that they GIVE people UNDESERVED TRUST, which leads to being unsafe.

Children raised in bullying environments often grow up to respond to adult bullying experiences, in the same ways as do adult kidnap victims or POWs. Adult and children, kidnap victims or POWs – change their behaviors so that they accommodate or co-depend the abusive guardian, in order to survive in the frightening environment.

They often take this over-accommodating behavior, which is a form of super-fast bonding being co-dependent – into most arenas of their adult lives.

This type of co-depending or fast, pressured-bonding, when it's in a kidnapping environment, was first called the "Stockholm Syndrome", since it was observed among kidnapped hostages in a Stockholm, Sweden, bank.

THE FIRST SET OF RESULTS:

When a child survives to the age of 18 and legally "escapes", they have had years of conditioning in:

- Fear of authority figures.
- Having a lack of assertiveness and self-protective skills (which is sometimes referred to as a lack of "boundaries").
- Often believing they have to keep this abusive treatment secret – which postpones recovery.
- Having a deeply ingrained habit of GIVING to other people – as they did to the "guardian" – UNDESERVED TRUST.

THE FINAL RESULT:

Abuse continues to happen to these "Adult Children", when they are adults if they do not STOP giving UNDESERVED TRUST to other people.

For recovery, they must:

- Acquire assertiveness skills – the biggest one of which is learning to say "No!" to people - setting boundaries skills - to defend themselves from unsafe people.

- They must learn to distinguish levels of trustworthiness, in order to protect themselves like healthy adults do, and NOT do any more giving of UNDESERVED TRUST.

CODEPENDENCE Styles – Codependence Is a "Soft" Addiction

Codependence is looking OUTSIDE ONESELF for emotional pleasure, acceptance, protection, praise, validation – and by looking OUTSIDE ONESELF – codependence is an addiction, just like looking to feel pleasure from a drink of alcohol is an addiction.

Do a reality check

Doing an assessment of your "secret flaws" – part of the baggage you keep hidden and drag around with you, can tip you off to how you get involved in the different types of codependent relationships.

Have you ever, or do you often:

- Want to be RIGHT – which entails some judgment of other people, and may entail "perfectionism".

- Want to feel like the SMARTEST person in the room – this can entail being sort of a nerd-show-off.

- Want to be LIKED – this entails being a "pleaser" to other people and doing what makes THEM pleased.

- Want to feel SUPERIOR – sort of like feeling like you are more "together" than some victim.

Look at Some Common Types of Codependence

Keep in mind that codependence is when two personalities "merge" emotionally, to get needs met that they do not attempt to get met ON THEIR OWN – this dependency is addictive.

THE URGE TO MERGE FOR POWER OR PROTECTION – a codependence style

Many people in adult children of Alcoholics and other dysfunctional families, have grown up in environments where humiliating was a TOOL used by caretakers to make kids be quiet and "toe the line" – a method of disciplining for control.

The lasting damage from having one's self esteem pummeled so often, is that one feels unworthy, or even feel like an "imposter" when something good happens to you – as if you are undeserving.

Feeling undeserving because you were raised around PERFECTIONISM, is not the same as living with "survivor's guilt" – where you feel guilty that you are alive because someone you were close to died and you lived. This is DIFFERENT.

FEELING DEEPLY FLAWED is often one of the legacies that come from a dysfunctional family that keep up the "perfectionist façade." Such households have adults who are constantly finding fault with kids – pointing it out.

Kid don't know enough to know that there IS NO PERFECTION – and that all the bad things that happen, all the mistakes that are part of learning, and all the actions that are blamed as their "fault" – "Look what you made me do!" – are all unskilled adults' behaviors relying on PASSING THE BLAME.

An "adult child's" solution to feeling deeply flawed can be to align themselves with someone else who they think is NOT deeply flawed, and hope it rubs off on them – COMPENSATION.

Two real-world examples may illustrate this drive to get and keep status, in a sick – or even criminal – manner – and both examples involve female attorneys, which is quite appalling.

FIRST EXAMPLE:

In January 2014, in Seattle, WA, journalists revealed the arrest of a male practicing attorney who had been committing rapes, and also exposed the fact that the wife – a practicing attorney – had been complicit in concealing his rape activity – his crimes. # # #

SECOND EXAMPLE:

This female attorney represented battered women in their cases against their batterers, in local court. This made her feel "superior' to her unfortunate clients. The reality was that she was a victim of domestic abuse too. She was emotionally battered in her own home, and was a covert alcoholic, to try to avoid looking at her problems. The husband had an administrative job, and had been verbally abusive – doing verbal put-downs – his entire working and professional life. He was a Class I. Bully. His 4 children would not speak to him or visit him or come to his house, except for rare exceptions, of maybe once a year to see their mother.

He trained his three dogs to ATTACK people, and would walk down his street with the dogs off-leash, and give them the command to "ATTACK!", on women and children who were walking down his street. One woman jogger reported him, and one father whose son was mauled on the thigh, reported him. There had been more than 5 deliberate "biting" events within 30 months, but he would offer the victims MONEY to not report him. This way he got a DOUBLE "HIGH" – because (1) he got to "hurt' someone and make them smaller than him so he was taller than them, and (3) he got to demonstrate FURTHER DOMINANCE by being able to BUY THEM OFF by the power of his money.

His wife had to hire other lawyers to try to save one dog from being put down after a biting incident. The judge ordered the dog put down, and the wife told the husband to get the dog out of the neighborhood, and they hid it in another town, and then moved it out of state. # # #

The women both BROKE THE LAW ALL THE TIME! Both stayed with the men for "perceived" status and "power" – even aggression – that the women LACKED.

Why did these women stay with these criminals?
UNREALISTIC THINKING ALLOWS PEOPLE TO MISTAKE BULLYING FOR STRENGTH THAT CAN PROTECT them! ALSO – the LONGER you stay with a Bully, the LOWER your WILL POWER!

Intimidating bullies destroy a victim's will
The more an Intimidating Bully or Abuser humiliates a Victim, the lower the Victim's will declines, to a level of sometimes becoming suicidal. Low will = low will to live.

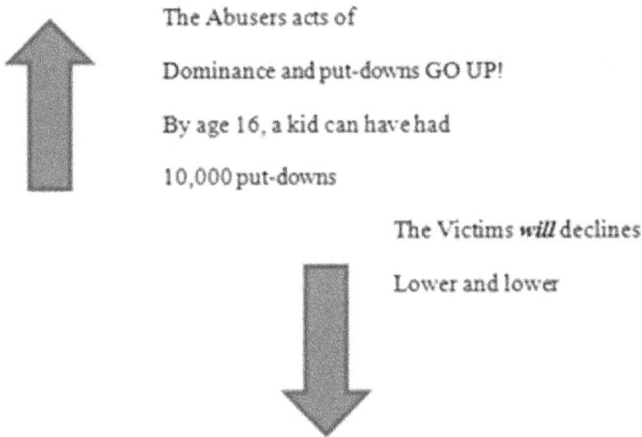

The Abusers acts of

Dominance and put-downs GO UP!

By age 16, a kid can have had

10,000 put-downs

The Victims *will* declines

Lower and lower

A victim's will declines with repeated humiliation.

EXAMPLE:
"As I was going through a long-distance divorce with my then husband – a nice guy who was grappling with a bad drinking problem that had caused him health problems – we had each found work on opposite coasts. It was natural that we each found new 'friends' too. His new love was my former best friend when we had lived on the West Coast in that city before. I found a new boyfriend who had his own tiny house, and a cat. I loved the cat. I

was tired of living in my apartment, and he gave me the impression that he had it much MORE TOGETHER than I did.

What he told me was how his family was in the Social Register – and they were – but he didn't earn enough to even make a donation to his old private school's annual contribution drive.

I was so insecure that the fact that I was a DAR – Daughter of the American Revolution, through a relative of Ben Franklin, that I thought HIS family was special.

His father had run through everything he ever made in publishing and was teaching at a community college to earn something to live on, in the town he lived in. My boyfriend was a 'builder' some of the time, and unemployed much of the time, and MY job in the corporate world, was what paid HIS mortgage. I found that he had previously relied on female 'boarders' as he called them, renting out two of his bedrooms.

It took me a couple of years, and giving him $5,000 over time, and hearing one of his previous 'boarders' say that he was a 'covert controller', for me to get up the backbone to move out. I desperately missed the cat.

I saw a therapist about the matter, and he kindly assured me that I would find other cats in my future. I didn't believe him at the time – but it was true.

I wept and wept over the cat situation, a lot more than losing my 'prestigious' boyfriend."

TIP:

When you have been raised to feel full of faults – and very unworthy – you may mistakenly believe that you have to hook up with someone ELSE who seems to have better prospects: someone who has the clout of an attorney, or the prestige of a Social Register member, or someone with a LOT of money - even if you don't like them. The inner person who feels riddled with flaws feels that they don't DESERVE to succeed on their own, so they must ATTACH themselves to someone else who feels entitled to succeed.

Of course, this person with more power, may also be a BULLY. And they may treat you badly.

LOVING DRAMA AND DISTRACTION – a codependence style

Drama codependence can be a ticking time bomb. Getting involved with a "drama-junkie" can be very difficult to get out, of, because it IS so dramatically engrossing. As one man said: "Our relationship was a train wreck, but if she had come back into my life – I would have got right back on the train."

There are plenty of highly functioning, even apparently "healthy" personalities, who have a strong desire to "merge with" or get deeply involved with – a person who has a LOT more problems than they do:

- Getting a "high" from the attendant drama.
- Feeling superior to the person with so many problems.

EXAMPLE:

"I was trimming grass on the edge of the yard that faced the main road, and this woman came walking down the street, and stopped to talk after I said a mumbled hello. She was very extroverted, and poured out her whole life story. So here was Tina, living down the road with a woman who was trying to help her get back on her feet. Tina smoked constantly, but had drastically cut down on her drinking. But she had not been able to control her irritable temper, so had lost a couple of jobs in hair salons.

Her life was a train wreck. Her drunken father had beaten her and made her sleep outside as a kid, until she ran away at 15 and got married. She pulled herself up by her bootstraps and qualified as a hairdresser.

She walked 5 miles to work – or until someone pulled over and gave her a ride to work – because she didn't have a car, and she refused to take the bus that did come somewhat near where she was living.

29

Someone had given her an old car, and she and a mechanic friend – she was mechanical – were putting it back to together. But she couldn't' afford the insurance. I and my spouse felt that making a gift of $300., directly to the insurance company, would be a good deed, and get her on her feet. I spoke to a local insurance agent and we arranged it.

That did all eventually come to pass. But before then, either she, or a drugged up friend, sent an email to my spouse saying: 'Tina had to go to London on an emergency and needs $3,000 to get home.' That was wild enough. Another time, we actually drove to where she lived, and HANDED her $150., to get some parts to finish the work on her broken car. And then 10 days later, she said we never gave it to her. Then another 10 days after that, she sort of 'remembered' and said that she had been wrong, and she was very, very sorry.

Needless to say we haven't done any more 'good deeds' of this sort. We just write a check to the Society of Prevention of Cruelty to Animals, instead, where there are no lies, no cons.

And of course, dealing with my 'helping' Tina, lasted about 3 months of extended time, or a solid month of my life that year – that I could have spent fixing my OWN messes. And of course, she never did say thank you. I learned that some of the dramatic types think that the world WILL bail them out – that such dramatic turns are natural. I'll skip getting involved again."

TIP:

Sometimes it is PARTICULARLY DIFFICULT extricate oneself from such a situation if one of the people involved is a BORDELINE PERSONALITY. The Borderline personality is famous for:

- Getting angry frequently and controlling others by threatening to "blow up!"
- The Borderline LOVES to do verbal put-downs.
- The Borderline HATES to be alone, and sticks to people like flypaper.

Examine the childhood family environment. If a parent was constantly leaning on a child making them into a "mini-adult" or "adulterating' them – then the person may feel the need to COPY their PAST BEHAVIORS and try to be in charge of someone who is going off the rails – because they did it childhood.

SHORT-TERM RESCUES – an occasional codependence style

A person can find themselves in a situation where they are behaving like a codependent and getting into everyone's business, due to a crisis situation. It may literally be at the scene of an accident, or some other event that has "high stakes' or some survival pressure involved.

This is what attracts a lot of "savior" people, such as some attorneys – it's the FINGER-IN-THE-DYKE SYNDROME, where for a brief time, you are convinced that you are the only person that pulls things together.

EXAMPLE:

"One Saturday morning I was driving a back road to return to my condo, and the road wound by a lake, where people did a lot of rubber-necking at the boats on the water. Two vehicles ahead of me, I saw a pick-up truck hit a small dog that went airborne and landed on the side of the road. The car ahead of me slowed, but did not pull over.

I pulled over. I then started bossing the crowd that had gathered on the grass at the edge of the road, into telling me whose dog it was. The owners were on vacation, and the dog sitter had obviously made a mistake and let the little dog out. The dog was still alive, although now somewhat bloody. I asked a guy nearby if he knew where there was a vet open on a Saturday. He knew the dog's owners, so I directed him to hold the dog in his jacket, and get in my car, and direct me to the vet. A very LONG drive later, we arrived at the vet's and they were able to save the dog.

I got a Christmas card from the entire family expressing their heart-felt gratitude that someone had saved their beloved family member – the little dog. I was touched.

But I did not go drive over to meet them or ever see the dog again.

If this had happened on a weekday when I was driving on my way to work, I would NOT have pulled over and stopped. It was only because it was a Saturday and I could spare the time, that I helped out."

The PLEASER - a codependence style

Many people who are "pleasers" when you finally see them in grown-up form, didn't necessarily start out with that personality, or those inclinations, Their family of origin had NEED of a kid who would be "pleasing" when the rest of the family needed it.

Famous performers are evidence of the ability they learned and refined in childhood, to please or "entertain', deeply depressed or mentally ill parents. Comedian Jim Carrey has spoken about how his family was financially destitute after his father lost his accountant job, and the family had to sleep in their car. They ended up cleaning offices at night – kids and parents. Jim Carrey became very, very funny – and helped lighten the mood.

Tony award winner Nathan Lane is a comedian and actor who had a severely depressed mother, and he was the only one taking care of her, so he learned how to make her laugh. Judging from his clown face – half tragically sad as well as funny – it was a high price to pay to learn to do this.

The classic of all time is Charlie Chaplin, who with his brother, tried to keep their mentally ill mother in enough food and shelter so she wouldn't have to be institutionalized for her mental or emotional illness. Charlie Chaplin was one of the greatest comedians who ever lived – and had his childhood taken away from him – as he tried valiantly to support an adult who couldn't care for herself.

These talented comics are all "pleasers" because it was required of them – for their fractured families to survive their circumstances without becoming even more unhappy and sinking even lower into depression and malfunction.

EXAMPLE:

"I was the oldest child in a family with three younger siblings, and a mother who had been given terminal diagnosis of cancer. The family forced me into being a caretaker – or codependent – from doing all the younger kids' homework, to driving with my mother to get her funeral urn, and a long list of inappropriate tasks for a 13 year old kid. With an alcoholic father who enjoyed traveling (more chance to drink and more chance to cheat with other women), I was 'in charge' a lot of the time.

This worked out for me in school – chosen as a leader for many activities in student government – and later worked out for me in the work world where I would do anything to get the job done, so was well rewarded in high-risk industries, and made a little bit of industry 'history' with some of my achievements.

In my PRIVATE life, however, this all worked against me. I had had a 'friend' who was my best friend's brother, but I did not feel romantic about him. Eddie didn't take any hints from me, and went so far as to propose and embarrass us both. I told him I couldn't abandon my dying mother and younger siblings. His roommates, a married couple, both sat me down on a curb on the street one day and tried to INTIMIDATE me into marrying Eddie, because he loved me so much. They didn't care about ME. They just wanted him OUT of their apartment.

A few years later I didn't do much better, in that I fell for a sweet, smart, sensitive, man, who had been wounded in Viet Nam, and who was illegitimate, so he felt insecure. One of my brothers really liked him, so I eloped with him. We were great friends and good lovers for more than a decade, so that was a success. But we didn't keep our original agreement about being honest about our outside e affairs in our open marriage. I got 'surprised' to find underwear under the driver's seat that was not MY underwear, among other things. We eventually divorced.

But I went on to have one more codependent relationship where I was 'fronting' emotionally and doing all the heavy lifting, even with HIS friends. They were neat people, and they were actually rooting for me to leave him. Even his next door neighbor told me that I could do better and I was still young enough to start over.

Talk about the universe sending me signals!

I finally STOPPED being someone else's CONSOLATION PRIZE, and lived alone until I could figure out what type of person might be good for ME – and it was a very DIFFERENT type of person from the broken-winged types that I had been choosing before."

QUIZ – Your Boundaries

- Do you sleep with the first person who says to you, let's have sex?
- When was the last time you told a person "NO!"
- Have long has it been since you cut off a person who was talking too long on the phone?
- Have you ever HUNG UP on someone on the phone while they continued to talk?
- Have you ever been in a public space and seen someone whom you knew would talk to too much, and have you EVER said: "Hi, I can't talk now" and kept walking?
- Have you ever just turned your back on someone in public who was droning on and walked away?
- Do you give $40 to the first person who pressures you to do it? Street person or collecting for a gift at work?
- When was the last time someone "took advantage" of you – when you gave undeserved trust?
- When was the last time you returned a product you bought, to a store and got a refund?
- How "late" can a person be who is meeting you somewhere? 20 minutes? 30 minutes? 45 minutes? An hour?
- How many times can someone break a coffee date with you? Once? Two times? Three times?
- Do you have a taser or pepper spray or a portable alarm? Under what conditions would you have a taser or a portable alarm?
- Do you walk alone at night?
- When you have to go visit an intimidating or abusive person, do you take another person with you to psychologically change the dynamic to make yourself more safe?

Childhood Trauma Types Can Lead To Having No Boundaries

Trauma victims - kids and adults – react to the injuries they lived through by trying to prevent recurrence of what they endured, in one of three major ways. Sometimes people will flip back and forth between TWO styles of reaction, but usually ONE STYLE predominates.

WOUNDS FROM CHILDHOOD OR ADULTSHOOD, ARE HEALED BY RESPECT, AS FOLLOWS:

- Victim is hurt and humiliated – WOUNDED so WILL declines.
- Victim needs to be WITNESSED to start rebuilding WILL.

Don't dwell too long in the "getting sympathy'" zone – it does NOT HEAL the wound.

The humiliation wound is HEALED by RESPECT; recognition comes from volunteer or paid WORK.

The trauma victim styles are:

- This trauma victim type isolates and hides. They have emotional damage that is sometimes called somatic, such as some non-physical extreme traits of Aspergers or a bit of being compulsive, or schizoid. Hiding in addiction is also common. They can become obsessed in thinking, doing, learning, being workaholic – and usually avoid most people. This type does not speak out, and tries to "fly under the radar" in life to not get attacked again.

- This trauma victim type tries to be a "pleaser" with people, and is afraid of making anyone angry at him/her or disappointed in him/her. This type often looks to others to protect them – and they are usually quite late in adulthood in developing skills for themselves, to keep safe. This trauma type is often re-victimized during adult life.

- This trauma victim type tries to push around other people – sometimes with charm and even humor – but constantly seeks to be in control of not just his or herself, but to have control over others.

This victim victimizes other people throughout their life. Sometimes it's covert bullying.

Examine yourself in two complex components:

- The degree to which each codependent LOOKS OUTSIDE THEMSELVES for validation, The degree to which codependents rely on other people's reactions give them their self worth; which is the behavior of all other ADDICTIONS – looking OUTSIDE to feel better, instead of inside for peace or relief from pain.

- The degree of EMOTIONAL INTENSITY that the codependence dynamic contains – such as low, moderate, or deeply attached like Siamese twins. Codependence is described in the psychology dictionary as a mutual dependence where two individuals are EMOTIONALLY dependent upon each other.

Therapist Judith Sills in her book "Get rid of your excess baggage", said that people have emotional drives to be "liked", or to "be right", or to "feel superior" to someone else, to "dominate other people", and there are many other emotional drivers.

An example of EMOTIONAL codependence in action

You are at a community meeting, for the first time, and a stranger to you, at the meeting, (and this can even happen if you go to a new ACoA meeting), comes up at the very end of the meeting and asks you to drive them home and says it's not far.

By their WAITING to CORNER you at the end, when others aren't around they are using SURPRISE as an intimidation tool. They already have a plan B in their heads, since they did GET to the meeting. But their Plan A would give them an EMOTIONAL HIGH, if they could INTIMIDATE you – giving them the emotional high feeling of having DOMINATED. If you are a person who has a high need "to be liked" – you may be afraid to say "NO" – and you may think that person won't LIKE you.

That person was not ever going to LIKE you – they just wanted the EMOTIONAL EXCHANGE where YOUR emotionally GIVING IN made THEM feel EMOTIONALLY POWERFUL.

That's an example of two people being emotionally dependent on each other.

Ways to strengthen and build up your will

Keep a little written script with you in your pocket or purse, and refer to it when someone you know wants to take advantage of you or intimidate you. Remember to say:

- I've got another commitment that I can't break.
- NO. That won't work for me today. Good luck.
- When you are completely SURPRISED, take a few moments:, say: "Give me a few minutes to think about that."

Someone can be pushing you to give them a ride when you had not planned on it – and they SURPRISED you with the request to INTIMIDATE you. You need to have a PROTECTION SCRIPT: "Sorry, I can give you 5 bucks toward a cab, but I'm too booked to drive you."

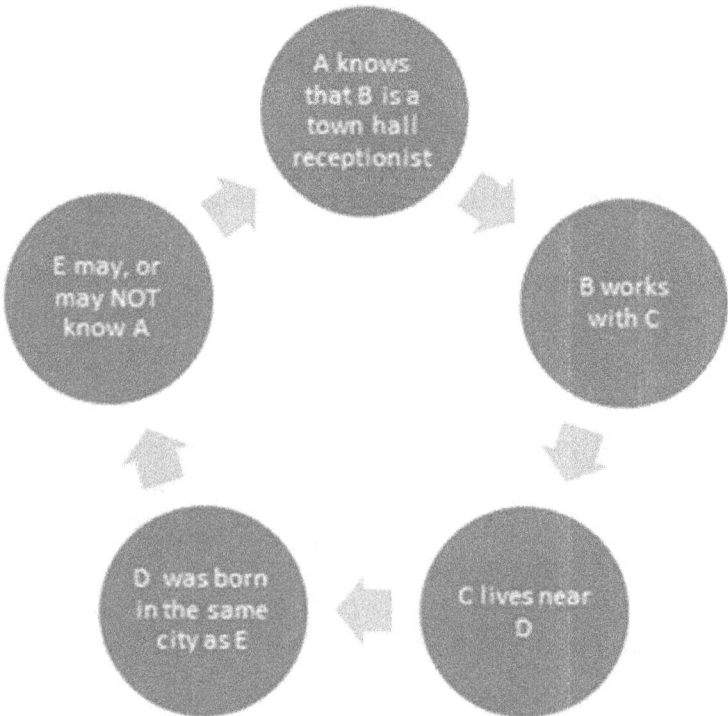

A knows that B is a town hall receptionist

B works with C

C lives near D

D was born in the same city as E

E may, or may NOT know A

People are naturally interdependent – NOT co-dependent

CODEPENDENCE CAN ARISE OUT OF FEAR OF BEING POWERLESS, OR REJECTED

The higher your codependence behaviors – the lower and fewer BOUNDARIES you have. Codependence is defined as when two people each get EMOTIONALLY dependent upon the other – enmeshed.

(A) Wants to dominate

1) Is pushy, doesn't say please or thank you

2) Feels GREAT when another person is SUBMISSIVE to them

(B) Wants to be liked

1) Fears a person geting mad at them if they say "NO"

2) Has a low WILL to protect one's time and self

CODEPENDENCE is about an IMBALANCE between two people.

QUIZ – 10 Ways To Be Codependent

CIRCLE "Y" FOR YES, OR "N" FOR NO, ON THE FOLLOWING TEN
WAYS TO BE CODEPENDENT

- **Y/N** At anytime have you let someone else have a "sympathy-high" off of you, and while you got nothing back?

- **Y/N** At anytime has someone extracted attention BIG-TIME from you and had a "pity-party" off of you as an audience, and used you for "consolation"?

- **Y/N** At anytime have you let someone have a "drama-high" off of you, when they extort attention about "their crisis"? When a person takes more energy FOR themselves and is taking this energy FROM you, by you allowing it you are being codependent. Others may suck more energy from you than you get back (like a highly extroverted person versus an introverted person).

- **Y/N** Have you let someone bully you into doing something you do NOT want to do?

- **Y/N** Have you ever let, or do you often let, someone do a "dominance high" on you – so that they have their WAY – and you do NOT, to avoid making a "scene" or having an argument? Meeting their "desires – no matter how unhealthy theirs may be – before meeting your own desires, is codependent.

- **Y/N** Have you been in any relationship where you do NOT get back what you give out? If you feel ANGER – it is a clue that the relationship is UNEQUAL – that you are giving more than they are, which is codependent.

- **Y/N** At anytime do you find yourself trying to "over-control" a situation?

- **Y/N** At anytime have you let yourself be manipulated – allowing yourself to be used by someone externally for purposes that you did NOT OFFER, that you do NOT think you are being "paid" enough for?

- **Y/N** At anytime you can't relax or can't "trust" others not to "try something", do you take control?

- **Y/N** At anytime did you feel superior to another, because of your "good deeds"?

Intimidating bullies destroy a victim's will

The more an Intimidating Bully or Abuser humiliates a Victim, the lower the Victim's will declines, to a level of sometimes becoming suicidal – low will = low will to live

Beware of sympathy attention interrupting recovery from humiliation, low and damaged will and wounds

WHEN VICTIMS ARE HIT OR HUMILIATED, THEIR WILL IS WOUNDED. REPAIR COMES FROM BEING WITNESSED, THEN MOVING ON TO "WORK"; WHICH GROWS RESPECT, & WILL, AND HEALS HUMILIATION. (Sympathy may feel good – but DOES NOT HEAL the wound.)

Learning Levels of Trust, Don't Be a Victim

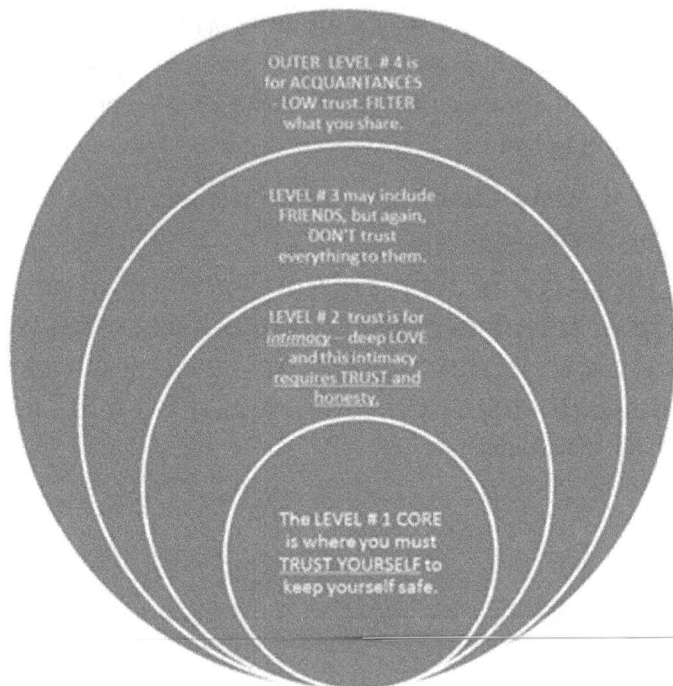

OUTER LEVEL # 4 is for ACQUAINTANCES - LOW trust. FILTER what you share.

LEVEL # 3 may include FRIENDS, but again, DON'T trust everything to them.

LEVEL # 2 trust is for *intimacy* – deep LOVE - and this intimacy requires TRUST and honesty.

The LEVEL # 1 CORE is where you must TRUST YOURSELF to keep yourself safe.

- OUTER LEVEL #4 is for acquaintances, You must FILTER how much you trust them.
- LEVEL #3 is for friends, but again, you may not trust them with EVERYTHING.
- LEVEL #2 is for intimacy – deep LOVE - and this intimacy requires high TRUST and honesty.
- LEVEL #1 CORE is the most important – you must TRUST YOURSELF to keep yourself safe.

Forgiveness

Forgiveness is complex, but for purposes of recovering quickly, focus on three clarifying points:

ONE - The person who has hurt you, or continues to hurt you, is not looking for you to forgive them if they have not expressed remorse. In a one-sided relationship you are in it alone. This means step back emotionally and become disengaged from their insults or rage. To stay engaged only allows you to be hurt more and they may not ever express remorse.

TWO - If you disconnect emotionally – reduce your "emotional investment" in the interactions with a person who has harmed you or continues to harm you, you reclaim your energy for your own recovery and increased happiness. The fastest way to do this, is to do a "general forgiveness" that basically acknowledges: "Everyone has some flaws. I am not going to focus on what was done to me in the past, I am forgiving what was done in a "general pardon" and am not after revenge or apologies. This attitude and action choice is: to forgive to more forward. Keep an emotional attitude of: "Live, and let live."

THREE - To be able to arrive at focusing on you moving forward in recovery to be the successful survivor you can be, it is helpful to go examine (1) the extent of your grief, and relieve and express the grief; (2) understand that anger is a signal to you to protect yourself; and (3) avoid being sucked down the drain of hatred – it can consume so much energy that it can destroy a person.

(1) Grieving

Anyone who has ever lost whom they loved, needs to have the luxury of time to weep and grieve out the pain, or the heart can't cope. There is enormous loneliness that each child feels, when they feel unlovable. Grieving, relieves the painful feelings, so a child's enormous burden doesn't have to keep being dragged alongside the adult. After the grieving, a person can move forward to discover strengths and abilities – leaving behind, the abusive experiences.

(2) Anger

Anger, in short bursts, like fear, in short bursts is s signal for self protection that you need to defend yourself. Short bursts of anger can also motivate someone to change, and do better for themselves.

Most children who were abused painfully remember that they could not defend themselves when they were young. They can use that memory to learn and equip themselves with abilities to protect themselves as adults. Others, do not change much, and some adults some people compulsively hold onto anger, because they think it will defend them. Holding on to anger for a long time is not healthy.

(3) Hatred

Anger added to bitterness can cause hatred. There's a limit to how long anyone can keep hatred going, because it only seems like strength. Hatred really is rather like a tick sucking out your blood, and depletes your energy, which is why hatred is a self-destructive emotion. Hatred also leads to violence.

FOR YOUR FASTEST RECOVERY: Forgive to more forward. Keep an emotional attitude of: "Live, and let live."

HAND-OUT on Forgiveness

TRUST yourself and FORGIVE yourself.

Emotional pain can linger from events in the distant past, where we felt we were not protected adequately by our parents or caretakers, or not even adequately protected by God.

Arriving at a state of forgiveness means that we NO LONGER FEEL WE ARE OWED ANYTHING for the hurt that was inflicted upon us.

Inflicting hurt upon people has been handled in many different ways in our past. As recently as 1900, among the Comanche tribe in the United States, if a tribe member raped a tribal woman, other members of the tribe killed him right then. It was a rule of the tribe.

In England, in Anglo-Saxon times, the Saxons had a system of fines for EVERY cruel thing that could be done to another person, where a person paid the fine for their action. So if one person murdered another, they would "pay" or "for-give" by, say, having an arm or a leg cut-off.

This type of "forgiveness" means that you do not feel OWED any longer by this person for their past harm to you. It DOES NOT mean that you have to extend any trust or closeness to them.

Many of the people who harm children or other adults, have themselves been severely harmed, demeaned – damaged – and some are truly mentally ill. It is impossible to expect that people so damaged, will ever achieve "okay" behavior, and so it is equally impossible to imagine ever having close, trusting relationships with them. You can FORGIVE them for the past harm done to you – but you DO NOT have to EVER trust them again.

One female physician, took care of her younger siblings, when her mother ran away from her father. Within a few years, the father started sexually abusing her. She grew up, was married twice, had a daughter, and was a successful physician for many years. At one point, she went back and saw her father and told him she understood he had been emotionally ill and she forgave him for what he had done, and she told him that she was never going to see him again, because she couldn't think of anything useful he could contribute to her or her child's lives in the future.

TRUST yourself and FORGIVE yourself

Before you can forgive anyone else, you must forgive yourself for not having been able to protect yourself when you were hurt. We blame ourselves, and sometimes others blame us and say it was our own fault, but we usually INTERNALLY blame ourselves, no matter how young and powerless we were.

TRUST yourself and FORGIVE yourself.

Things To Say To Forgive Yourself

After you choose something to say to yourself, sit quietly for two minutes afterwards to let the idea settle.

- "I forgive myself for judging, feeling guilt, or for feeling stupid about (whatever happened)."

- "I forgive myself for my negative thoughts and feelings when things didn't go as I wanted them to in my work, that I was counting on."

- I forgive myself for carrying a grudge against my father ignoring my requests to help me with my homework."

- "I forgive myself for being angry with God when I said the wrong thing in church or Sunday school, and got criticized for it."

- "I forgive myself for being angry at God because of what my parent(s) did.'

- "I forgive myself for my negative thoughts and feelings about my parent(s) (caretakers) decisions."

Author's Bio

Ann Ford

Ford has a M.S. in counseling psychology, Phi Kappa Phi, and did post-graduate work and instructed at Johns Hopkins in adult learning styles. She has counseled over 300 clients, primarily as part of large business downsizings, helping people through grief, forced change, and how to start over. She has lectured to university psychology departments on the cycle of domestic violence, taught court-ordered DV offenders new skills and taught the domestic violence cycle to incoming police recruits, and has conducted seminars nationally on sexual harassment.

She's been published in many publications, has been a columnist, and in recent years has won a few literary awards, writing books on multiple subjects, including a children's book on Hiroshima.

She's been nominated for a broadcasting award from American Women in Radio and Television, and won a Communications Arts Award, for work in her first career, which was radio and television broadcasting.

48

BIBLIOGRAPHY

- IN TOUCH magazine, February 10, 2014.
- *"Diagnostic and Statistical Manual of Mental Disorders (DSM)"*, by the American Psychiatric Association.
- *"A Child called IT – One Child's Courage to Survive"* by Dave Pelzer.
- *"Running With Scissors"* by Augusten Burroughs, made into a movie.
- *"Miss America by Day"* is a book that recounts the nightmare-level experiences of former Miss America Marilyn Van Derbur.
- *"Get Rid Of Your Excess Baggage"*, by Judith Sills.
- *"The Dictionary Of Psychology"*, by Arthur & Emily Reber.

INDEX